Note to Parents and Teachers

The SCIENCE STARTERS series introduces key science vocabulary and concepts to young children while encouraging them to discover and understand the world around them. The series works as a set of graded readers in three levels.

LEVEL 3: READ ALONE
These books can be read alone or as part of guided or group reading. Each book has three sections:

• Information pages that introduce key concepts. Key words appear in bold for easy recognition on pages where the related science concepts are explained.
• A lively story that recalls this vocabulary and encourages children to use these words when they talk and write.
• A quiz asks children to look back and recall what they have read.

WHAT IS A SHADOW? looks at LIGHT. Below are some answers and activities related to the questions on the information spreads that parents, carers, and teachers can use to discuss and develop further ideas and concepts:

p. 4 *Why are some places dark all the time?* Ask children to think about places where light can't get in, e.g. inside a cave, cupboard, or box.

p. 6 *How else can you protect yourself from the sun?* You can wear a hat to protect your head, a T-shirt to cover your skin, and wear sunscreen to protect bare skin.

p. 11 *Can you guess what objects are by feeling them?* Ask children to think about how different senses help them to find their way in the day and at night.

p. 13 *Why do we have to be careful near candles?* Flames can burn and if you knock them they could start a fire. You could also mention that candles are useful in a power cut.

p. 15 *Will the silhouette change if the boy puts on a hat?* Yes. You could also ask if the silhouette changes if the boy moves nearer to or farther away from the light source.

p. 17 *What do you think happens to your shadow when you jump up in the air?* When your feet leave the ground, they no longer touch your shadow.

p. 19 *When do you cast the shortest shadows?* You cast the shortest shadows when the sun is highest in the sky—at noon. The longest shadows occur at sunrise and sunset.

p. 21 *When can't you use a sundial during the day?* When it is cloudy.

p. 23 *Which are transparent, translucent, or opaque?* Encourage children to make a chart sorting items into groups.

ADVISORY TEAM

Educational Consultant
Andrea Bright—Science Coordinator, Trafalgar Junior School

Literacy Consultant
Jackie Holderness—former Senior Lecturer in Primary Education, Westminster Institute, Oxford Brookes University

Series Consultants
Anne Fussell—Early Years Teacher and University Tutor, Westminster Institute, Oxford Brookes University

David Fussell—C.Chem., FRSC

CONTENTS

© Aladdin Books Ltd 2006

Designed and produced by
Aladdin Books Ltd

First published in
the United States in 2006 by
Stargazer Books
c/o The Creative Company
123 South Broad Street
P.O. Box 227, Mankato
Minnesota 56002

Printed in Malaysia
All rights reserved

Editor: Sally Hewitt
Design: Flick, Book Design
and Graphics

Thanks to:
• The pupils of Trafalgar Junior School and
St. Paul's C.E. Primary School for appearing
as models in this book.
• Andrea Bright, Janice Bibby, and Stephanie
Cox for helping to organize the photoshoots.
• The pupils and teachers of Trafalgar Junior
School and St. Nicholas C.E. Infant School
for testing the sample books.

**Library of Congress Cataloging-in-
Publication Data**

Pipe, Jim, 1966-
  Light / by Jim Pipe.
    Includes index.
    p. cm. -- (Science starters. Level 3)
  ISBN 1-59604-017-3
  1. Light--Juvenile literature. 2. Sun--
Juvenile literature. 3. Light sources--
Juvenile literature. I. Title. II. Series

QC360.P57 2005
535--dc22
                                   2005041817

Photocredits:
*l-left, r-right, b-bottom, t-top,
c-center, m-middle*
Cover b, 24 both, 25b, 26 both,
27ml & br, 28tr—Jim Pipe. Cover
tl & tm, 5r, 31 —Flat Earth.
Cover tr, 3, 13b, 15ml, 16tr, 18bl,
19bl, 31bcr—Photodisc. 2tl, 2bl,
4 both, 5r, 5c, 9bl, 11tr, 11ml,
12tr, 13t, 14tr, 20tr, 22b, 23tl,
31mr, 31bl, 31bcl —Corbis. 2ml,
11br, 15br, 16bl, 17 all, 19ml &
mr, 23br, 28b, 29ml, 29b, 30
both—Marc Arundale/Select
Pictures. 6tr, 7b, 14b, 22tr—DAJ.
6bl, 7tr, 21t, 31ml—Flick Smith.
10l— Comstock. 10r—Brand X
Pictures. 12tml—Select Pictures.
12b—Flat Earth. 15tr —Corel.
18tr, 21b —Stockbyte. 20b,
23mr, 25tr, 29tr, 31br—Ingram
Publishing. 27t —John Foxx
Images.

LIGHT

What Is a Shadow?

by Jim Pipe

Stargazer Books

LIGHT AND DARK

These two pictures show the same place. In this picture it is **light**. You can see trees and animals.

Light

Dark

Here it is almost **dark**. Without **light**, you can't see anything!

Places are dark when there is no light. When the sun sets, it gets dark outside. Why are some places dark all the time?

During the day, the **light** changes outside.
When the sun is low, the sky is **darker**.
When the sun is high, the sky is **lighter**.

Sunrise
The day starts to get light when the sun appears. This is called sunrise.

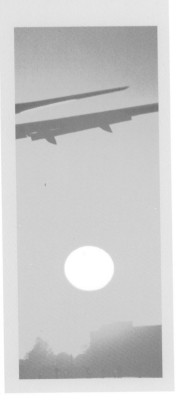

Noon
The sky gets lighter and lighter until noon. This is the middle of the day.

Sunset
Later in the day, the sun appears lower. When the sun has set, it is dark and night.

THE SUN

The **sun** lights up our day.
When it is cloudy, colors look dull.
When the **sun** shines,
colors look bright.

A sunny day can
cheer you up.
But the **sun** can
also harm you.

NEVER look
straight at the **sun**.
It can damage
your eyes.

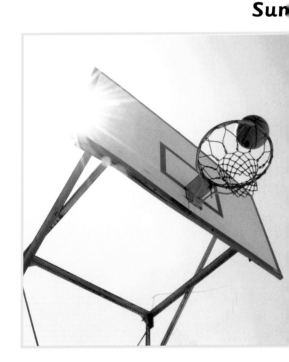

Sun

Hat

Sunglasses

T-shirt

Sunglasses protect your
eyes from bright light.
How else can you protect
yourself from the sun?

Heat from the **sun**
can burn your skin.
Rubbing sunscreen on your
skin helps to protect it.

On a hot day, don't
stay too long in the **sun**.
Play indoors or find
a place in the shade.

Sunscreen

In the shade

STARS AND MOON

The sun is a **star** just like the **stars** that twinkle in the night sky.

But the sun is much closer to Earth than any other **star**. That is why it is so bright.

Sun shines

Sun's light

Many groups of stars have names. This group of stars is Orion.

Remember this shape and see if you can spot this group of stars in the sky at night.

Group of stars

The earth is always spinning.
It spins all the way around once each day.

The sun can only shine on one side of the earth at a time. On this side it is daytime. On the other side it is dark and night-time.

Earth spins

Moon

The **moon** does not make its own light like the sun.

Moonlight is light from the sun bouncing off the **moon**.

DAY AND NIGHT

As the earth spins, it changes from **day** to **night** on your side of the world.

Day

Night

People cannot see things easily in the dark. So most people work during the **day** when it is light and sleep at **night** when it is dark.

Animals and plants also need the sun's light to live and grow.

Most animals are busy in the day, too. But some animals can see in low light. They hunt for food at **night**.

The big eyes of this leopard help it to see in the moonlight.

Plants need light from the sun to grow.

Sunflowers face the sun to get as much light as they can.

Leopard

Put on a blindfold. Ask a friend to put different objects on a table.

Can you guess what objects are by feeling them? Would it be easier to know by seeing them?

LIGHT SOURCES

During the day our light comes from the sun. It is a natural **light source**.

When it gets dark at night, we use manmade **light sources**.

Electricity powers the lights in your home and on the streets. This street is lit up by thousands of colored lights.

A flashlight is a manmade light source. Its power come from batteries.

Street lights

Ask an adult to light a candle for you. Watch what happens when the flame moves about, or flickers.

Why do we have to be careful near candles?

When things burn they give off light. Before electric lights were invented, people used candles as **light sources**.

Candle

Many people around the world still use fire as a **light source** as well as for cooking.

A campfire

LIGHT RAYS

Look at light shining through this window.

Can you see that the light travels in straight lines? These lines are called **rays**.

When you stand in the sun, you block the **light rays** with your body. This makes a dark patch on the ground. This is your shadow.

Light rays

Shadow

Because **light rays** travel in straight lines, they can't bend around objects.

A cave is dark because the **light rays** can't follow it as it twists and turns.

Cave

What are these shapes? When we see only the dark side of an object we see its silhouette.

This girl is drawing the silhouette of her friend on a board.

Will the silhouette change if the boy puts on a hat?

Silhouette

SHADOWS

Anything that blocks light rays makes a **shadow**. When you move, your shadow does too.

What is making the big **shadow** in this picture?

Shadow from the sun

Shadow from a light

This girl is making a big, scary **shadow** by standing near to a light.

When she moves away from the light, her **shadow** gets smaller.

16

Dog

Rabbit

These children are making shapes with **shadows**. They are using flashlights and some other light sources.

They stand near a wall to see the **shadow** clearly.

When you stand on the ground, a shadow always touches your feet.

What do you think happens to your shadow when you jump up in the air?

This boy is making his shadow as small as he can. He is crouching down on the ground.

LONGER AND SHORTER

As the sun moves across the sky, shadows get **longer** and **shorter**.

But the sun is not really moving. It's the earth that moves.

The sun appears to move because the earth is spinning around and around.

Earth spins like a globe

When the sun is low in the sky, your body blocks more of the sun's rays. You cast a **longer** shadow.

In the middle of the day, the sun appears high in the sky. You block less rays. So you cast a **shorter** shadow.

Early morning shadow   **Midday shadow**

At what times of day do you cast the longest shadows?

When do you cast the shortest shadows?

SUNDIALS

The sun divides each 24 hours into day and night.

We can guess the time by seeing where the sun is. We can also use shadows to tell the time.

The upright part of a **sundial** makes a shadow. As the sun changes position in the sky, this shadow points out the time.

Sunset

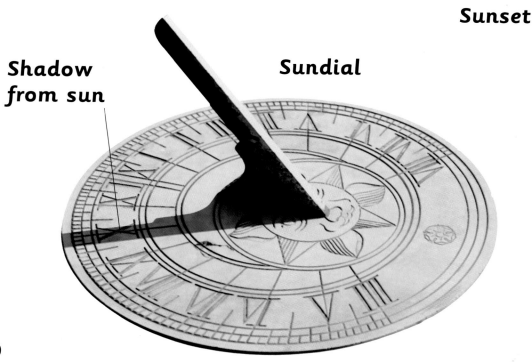

Shadow from sun

Sundial

This boy is making a **sundial**.
First, he puts a tall stick into the ground.

He marks the stick's shadow with a stone.
Every hour he marks the shadow again with
another stone. He writes the hour on each stone.

Tomorrow he can tell the time by seeing
which stone the sun's shadow points to.

A sundial does not work
at night as there are no
shadows from the sun.

When can't you use a
sundial during the day?

TRANSLUCENT AND OPAQUE

A glass window is transparent.
You can see right through it.

**Transparent
glass**

Some materials let some light
pass through them. But you
cannot see through them.
They are **translucent**.

Translucent curtains

Some objects do not let light through. We say these objects are **opaque**.

Opaque objects make shadows when they block light rays. An umbrella blocks most of the sun's light.

Opaque umbrella

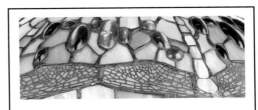

These pieces of colored glass are translucent.

Look at plastic candy wrappers, plastic bottles, wood, metal, jelly jars, and tracing paper. Which are transparent, translucent, or opaque?

THE SHADOW SHOW

Look for ideas about shadows.

It was early in the morning and the sun was low in the sky.

Inside, Chloe was reading the story of Peter Pan. She and her sister Clara were going to put on a shadow show with their cousins Ben and Sharon. Ben had said they should all think of ideas using shadows.

In the story, Peter Pan's shadow is stolen by Wendy's dog, Nana. Luckily, Wendy sews Peter Pan's shadow back on!

"That's a hard story to do," said Chloe.

"I agree," said Clara. "But it's a sunny day. Let's go outside and get some ideas!"

24

The girls put on their coats.
"The sun is very bright
today," said Clara.
"I wish I had my sunglasses."

The girls walked outside.
"Look how my shadow always touches my feet,"
said Clara. "Even when I run I can't lose it!"

"Your shadow makes you look taller," said Chloe.
"I'll remember that for our play."

Soon after, Ben and Sharon came over to play.

The sun was shining through the window.

"I'll show you how to make shadow shapes with your hands," said Ben. "This is a bird."
He moved his hands again. "And this is a dog."

"I can do better than that," said Chloe, picking up her fluffy dog. "You big cheat!" laughed Ben.

Later that day, they watched the sun going down. "Look at that pretty sunset," said Clara. "I guess that means no more shadows."

"We can use a lamp or a flashlight instead. Any light will do!" said Sharon.

"You're right. Look!" said Chloe, making a shape with her hand. "This lampshade lets the light through. It's translucent," said Clara.

"I know another trick," said Ben. "Look, our shadows can touch even though we're not."

"Now let's try to make some spooky shapes!" said Sharon.

The next morning, Uncle Justin arrived. He grabbed Clara and gave her a big hug.

"Look, it's a monster with four arms and two heads," shouted Ben.
Uncle Justin and Clara looked around—their two shadows were mixed together!

All the grown-ups went into the kitchen to chat. Ben said, "Let's get on with the show!"

"We made these puppets at school," said Sharon.

Sharon showed them the shapes cut from cardboard. Each shape was taped to a pencil so it was easy to hold.

The children thought about
what story they would do.
"Let's do Jack and the
Beanstalk," said Ben.
"A plant can be the beanstalk!"

"Who will be the giant?" asked Clara.

"I've got an idea," said Chloe.

Sharon's dad hung a sheet over
a line. Then he put a bright
light behind the sheet.

The grown-ups sat on the other side of
the sheet. Sharon's mom turned out the
main lights. The show was ready to begin.

The four children used a big
flashlight to help them read the
story in the dark.

Halfway through the story, Chloe stood up.
"Get down. You'll ruin it!" said Ben.

"I'm the *giant*," whispered Chloe.
"Next to a puppet, I'm huge!"
Everyone agreed that Chloe's
shadow made a great giant!

WRITE YOUR OWN STORY about shadows.
Make a list of the tricks you can play with
shadows and see which your friends can do.

Can you?	Helpful Hints
Mix two shadows	Make two shadows shake hands
Escape your shadow	Jump in the air
Fit inside a friend's shadow	Make yourself as small as you can
Make your shadow reach a place you can't go.	Touch the top of a tree's shadow.

QUIZ

When does the sun appear low in the sky?

Answer on pages 5 and 19

How does sunscreen protect your skin?

Answer on page 7

Why does a leopard have big eyes?

Answer on page 11

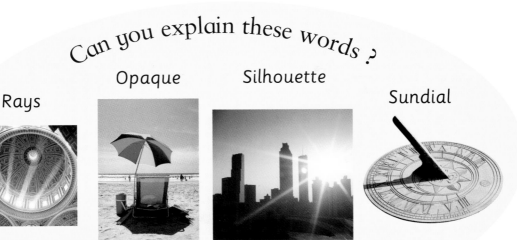

Can you explain these words?

Rays

Opaque

Silhouette

Sundial

Answers on pages 14, 15, 20, 23

INDEX